We hope you enjoy coloring this book.

Download some extra

free coloring patterns

and get news of upcoming books at

www.scribblepresscoloring.com/free-download

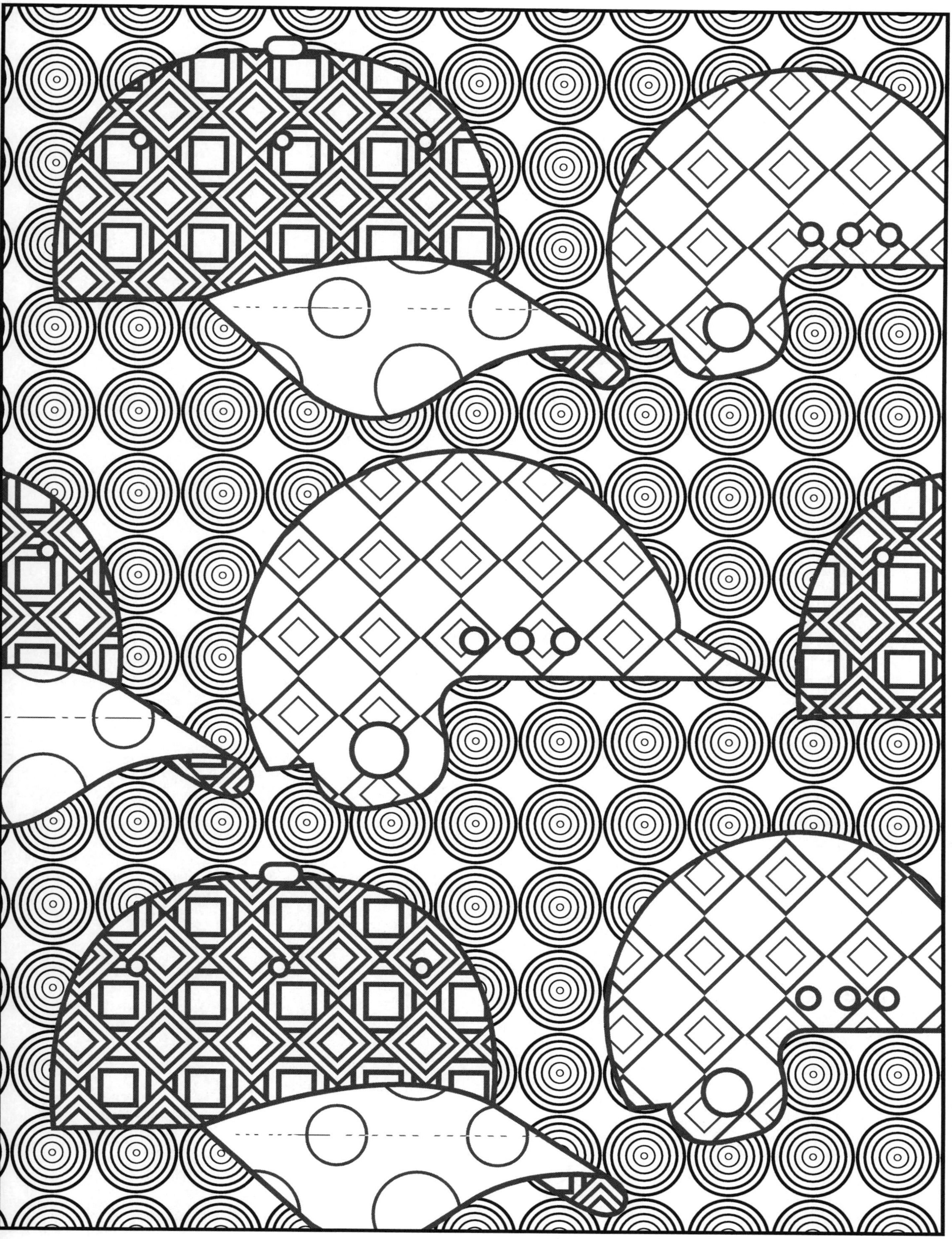

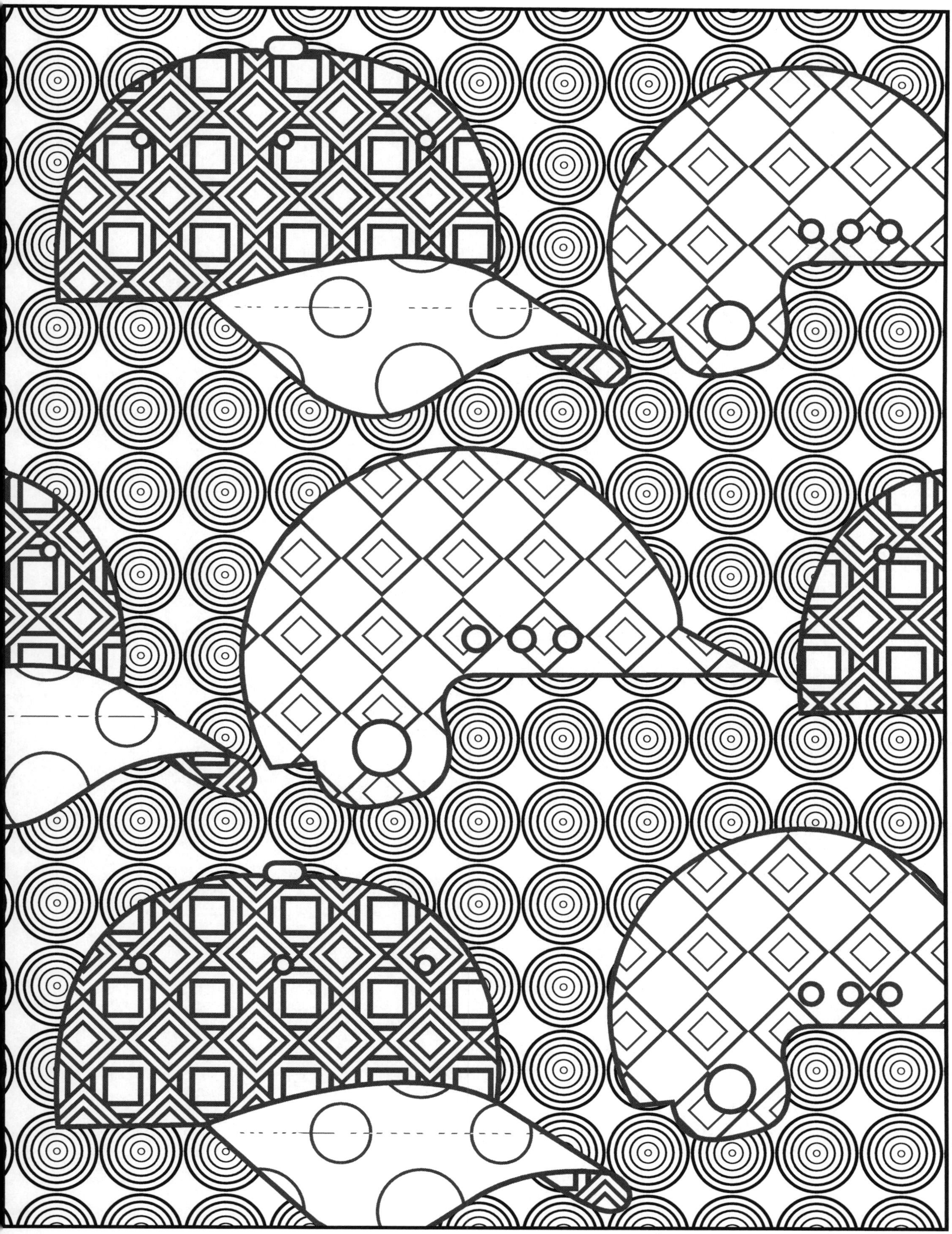

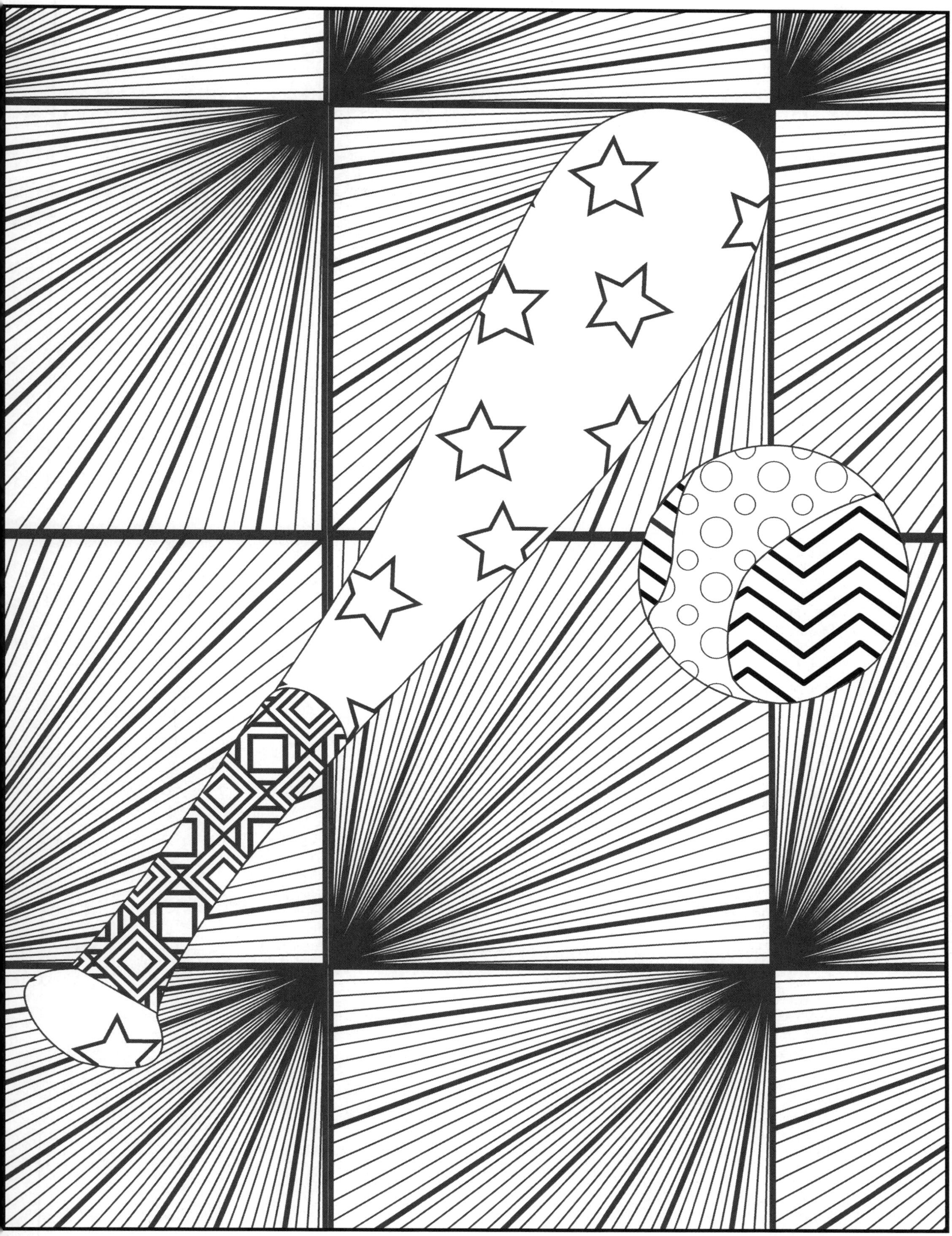

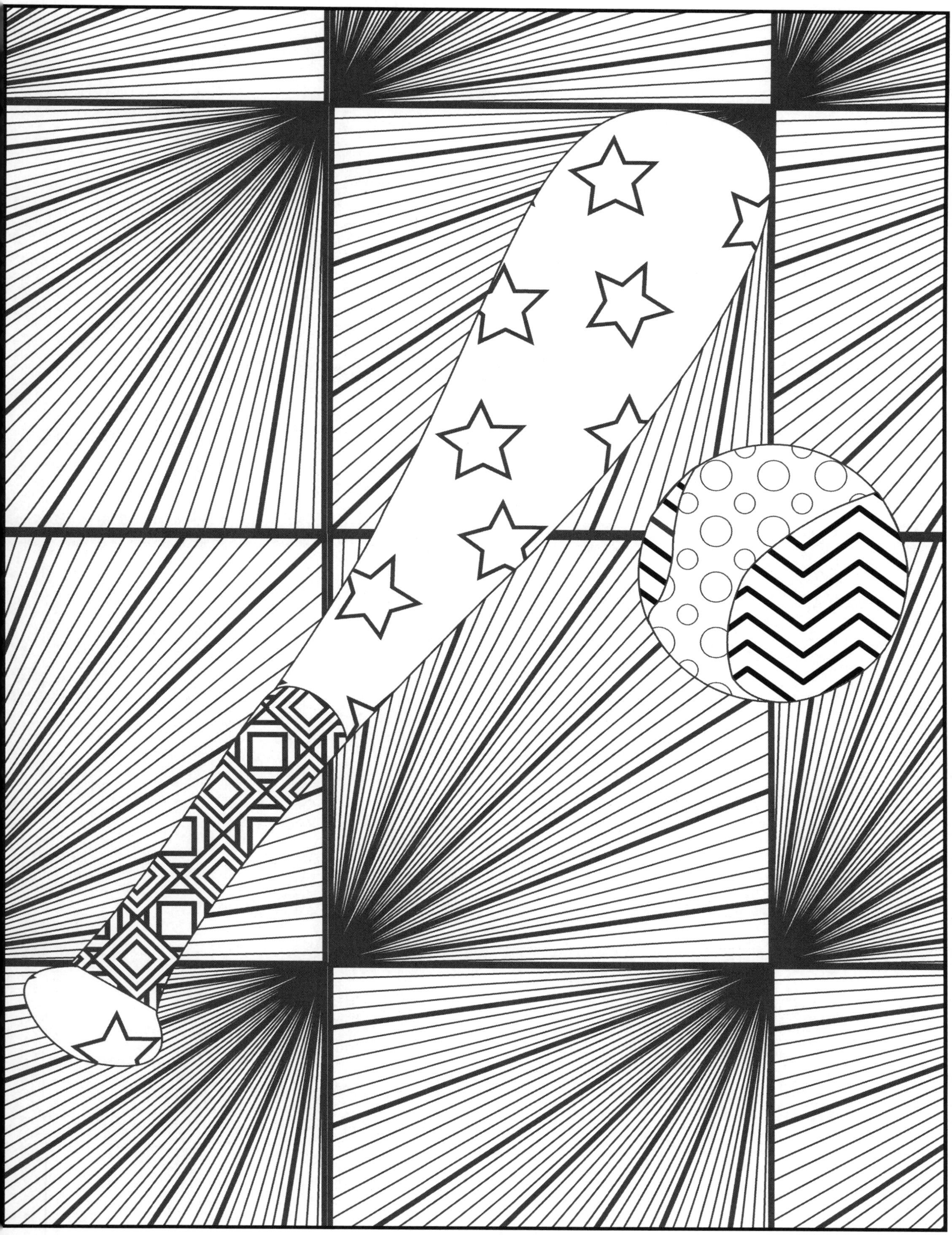

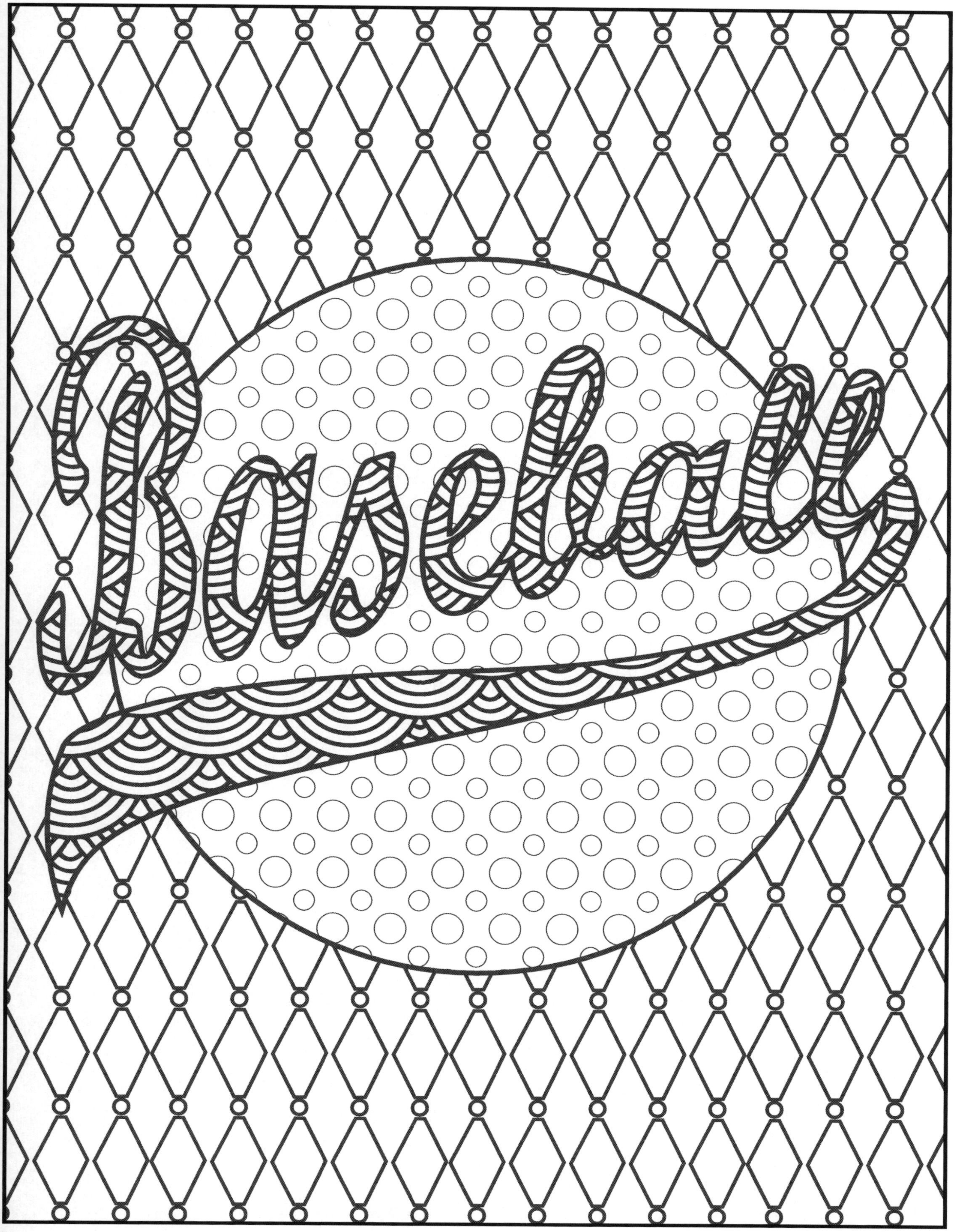
Baseball

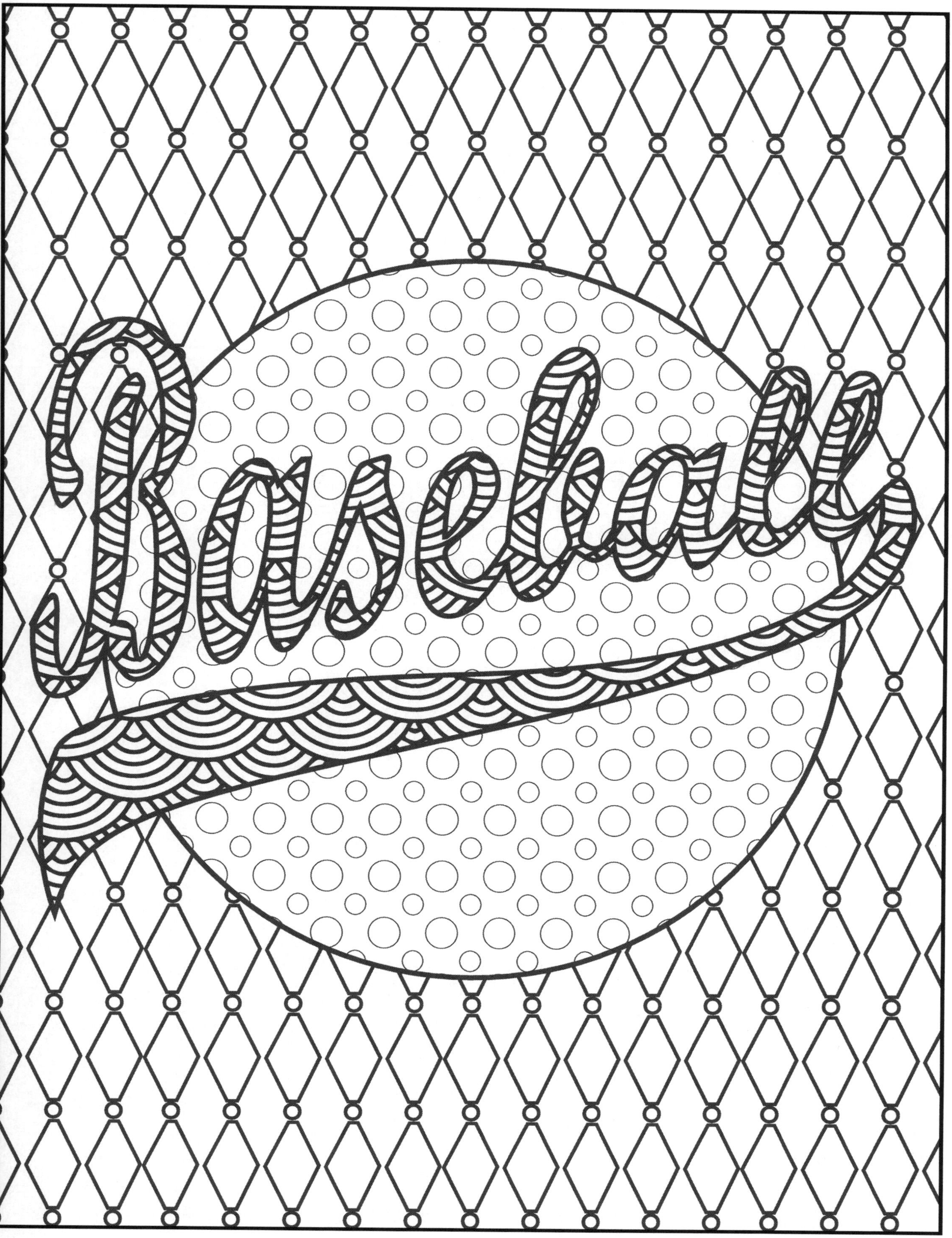
Baseball

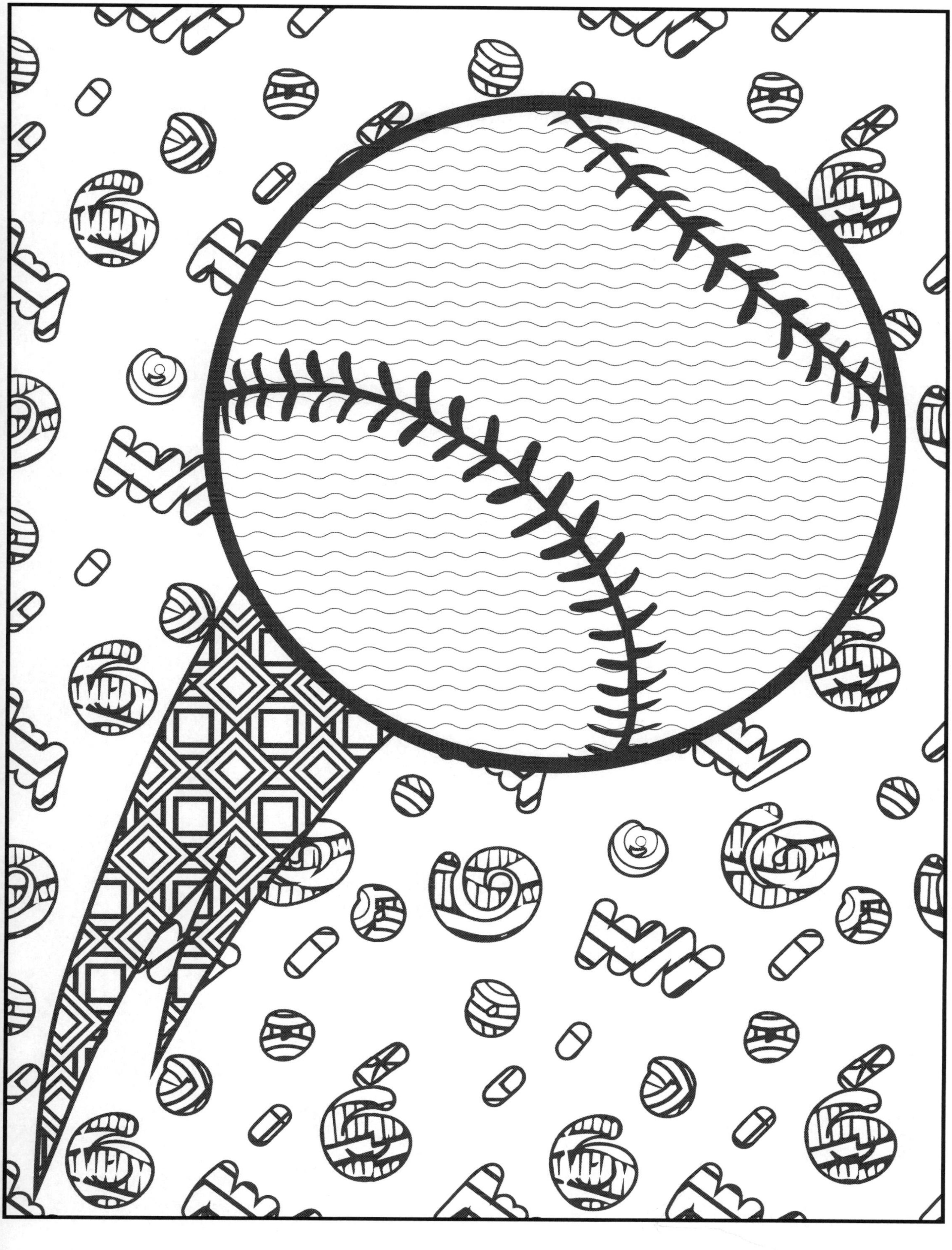

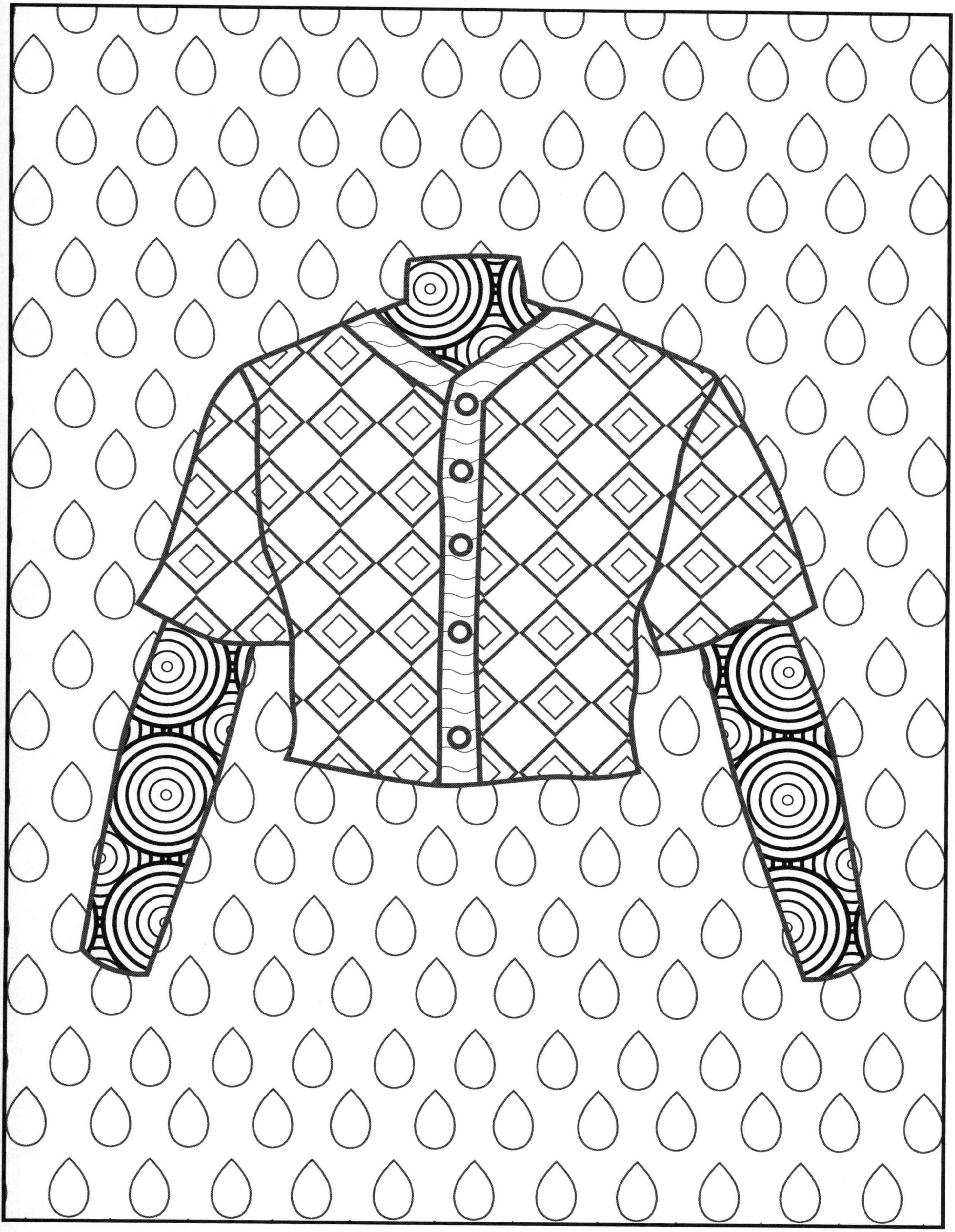

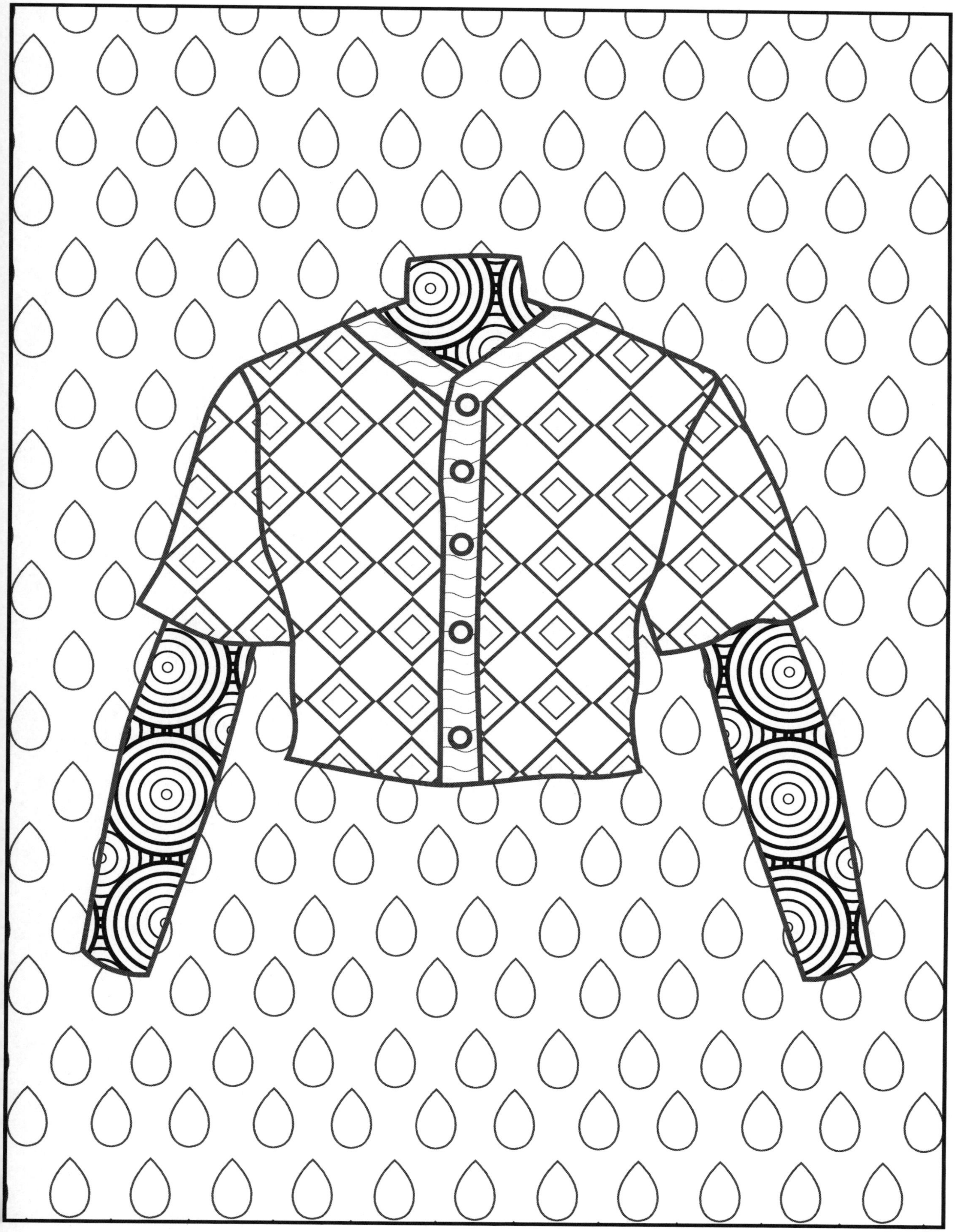

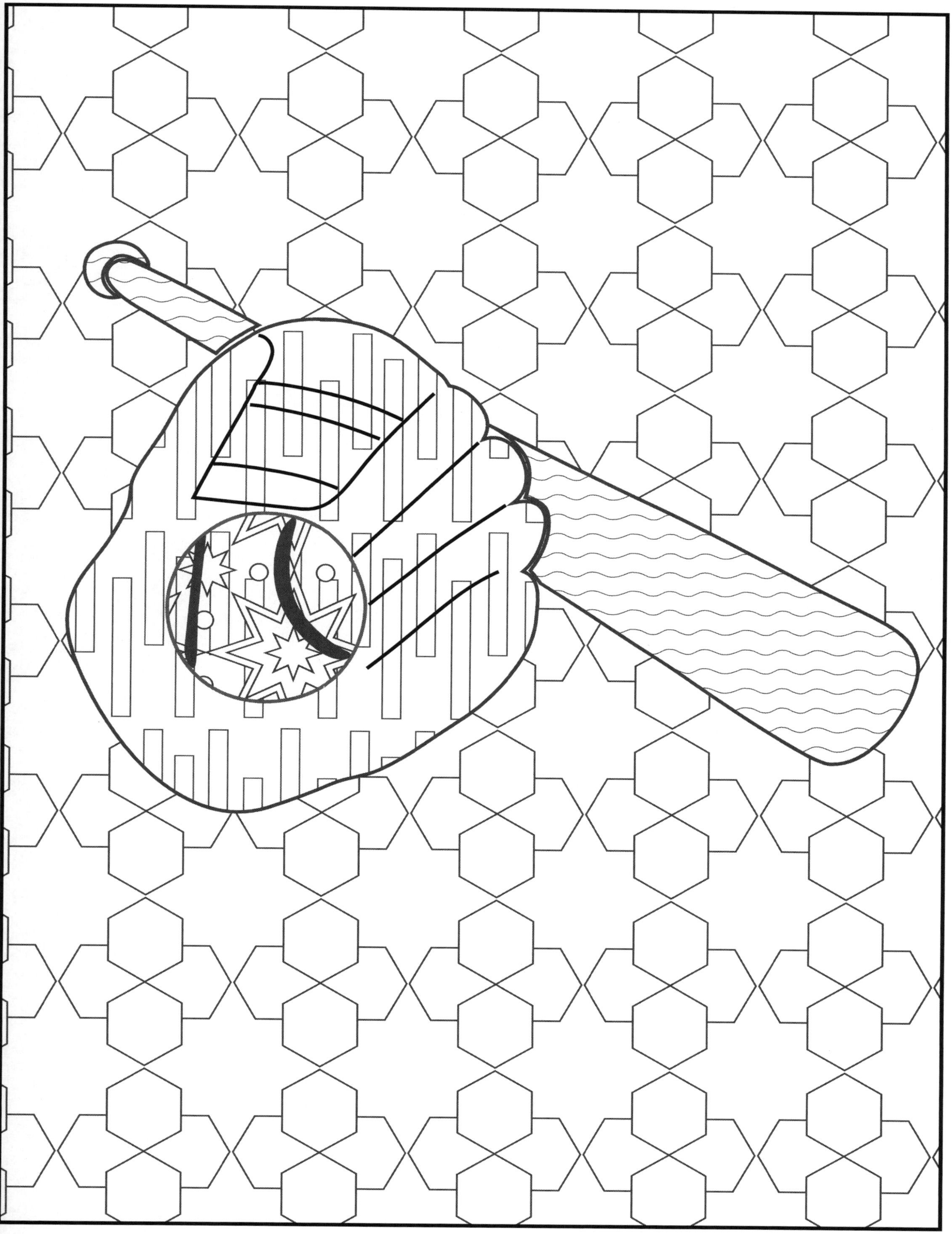

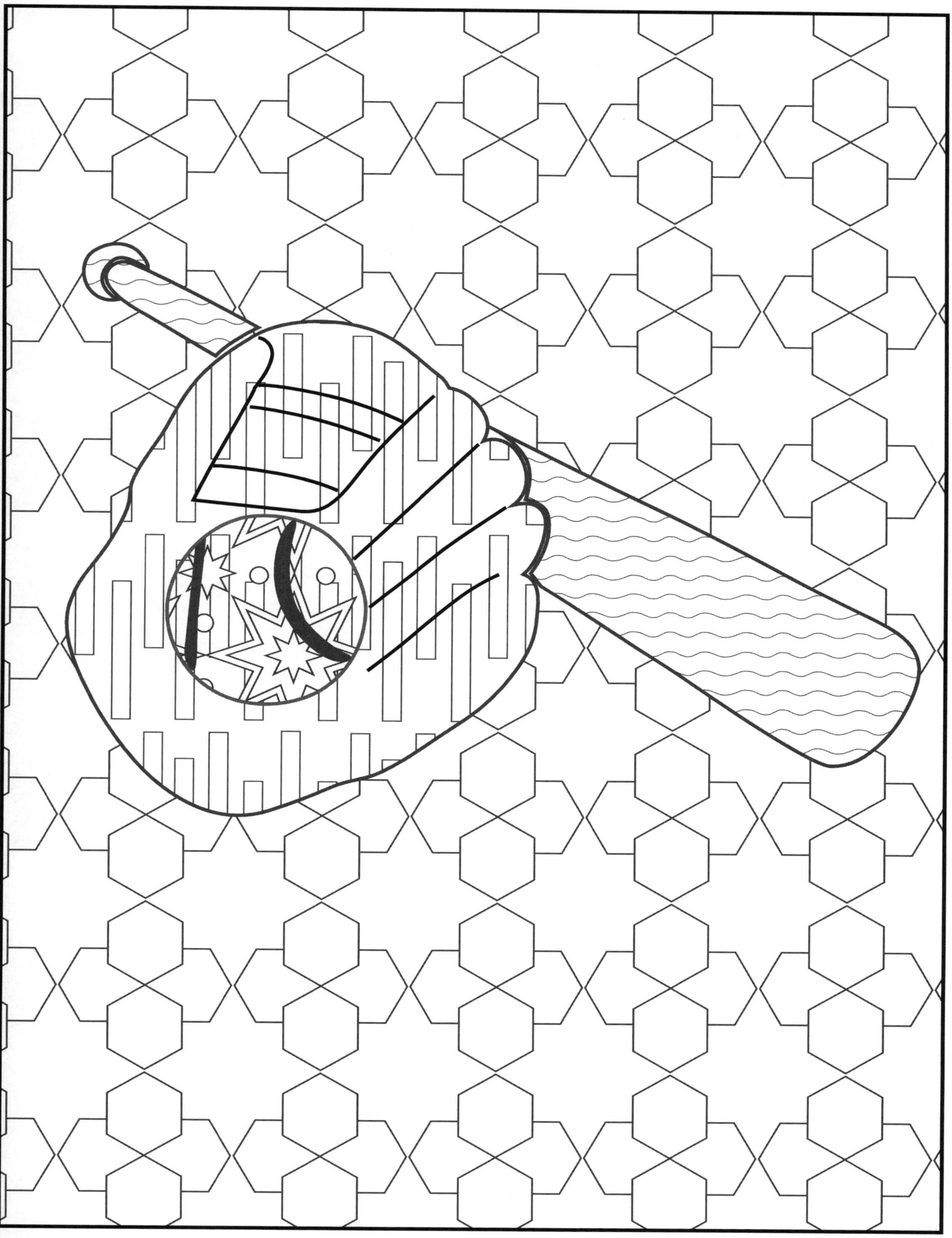

Made in the USA
San Bernardino, CA
26 March 2020

66376710R00035